Joy Journey

By *Loralie*

Poems, Hymns & Scriptures
for the Journey of Life

Poems and Illustration by Loralie Harris

Joy Journey
Poems, Hymns & Scriptures for the Journey of Life

Loralie Harris has devoted her career to creating colorful, friendly characters designed to bring on a smile and stir joy in the heart! Since their inception as a doodle on a hotel note pad, Loralie's fun, quirky characters have grown into a happy community spreading cheer around the world in poetry, fabrics and embroidery. Loralie's designs are featured on her Web site www.LoralieDesigns.com.

Published by:
Loralie Designs, LLC®
PO Box 475
Windsor, CO 80550

Unless otherwise identified, Scripture quotations used in this book are from the *New American Standard Bible®* (NASB) Copyright © 1960, 1962, 1963, 1968, 1971, 1972, 1073, 1975, 1977, 1995 by The Lockman Foundation. Used by permission. www.Lockman.org

Scripture quotations marked NIV) are taken from the *Holy Bible, New International Version®*, NIV®, Copyright © 1973, 1978, 1984, 2011 by Biblica™, Inc. Used by permission of Zondervan. All rights reserved worldwide. www.zondervan.com. The "NIV" and "New International Version" are trademarks registered in the United States Patent and Trademark Office by Biblca™,Inc.

Cover Art by Loralie Harris

ISBN:978-0-578-55360-3
Printed in the United States of America

Table of Contents

Joy Journey Fabric Collection

With a grateful heart I thank all those precious ones
who have accompanied me, encouraged me, and corrected
me on this journey. Teri, Connie, Sonny, Nancy, Pat,
Tim, Cari, Jan, Laura, Ruth, Allene, Sharon, Sandra,
and Jean. Thank you for your contribution and your
prayers. And to my precious husband of forty-five years,
Chuck, thank you for being my faithful support always.

INTRODUCTION

We are all on the journey of life with its
ups-and-downs and twists-and-turns. On my journey
I have been blessed to be able to create a world of
cheerful, friendly characters to be my sweet company
as I go. It has been my joy to share them with others
along the way in fabric and embroidery designs.

For *Joy Journey* I have created new characters and
also gathered some of my old favorites to adorn the
book pages, fabric and embroidery designs. It is a
patchwork of poems, hymns and Scriptures offered
to lift and encourage others as they have me.

It is my desire and prayer that the *Joy Journey*
fabric collection and book will be a cheerful world
of comfort and encouragement to all it may touch.

The plentiful open spaces can be used to note your
own thoughts. Purse-size, it will travel with you
everywhere to become a handy source of strength
and encouragment for yourself and for others.

Wishing you a pleasant journey,

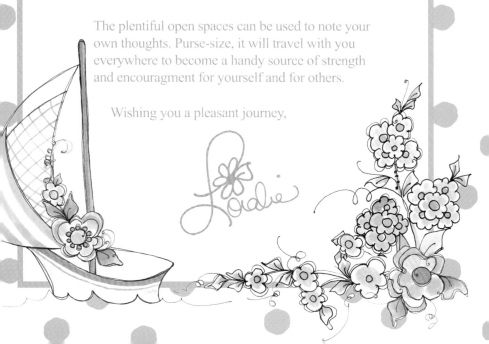

A joyful heart is good medicine.
Proverbs 17:22

Good Cheer

Scripture Pictures

JouRney

He knows the way I take;
When He has tried me,
I shall come forth as gold.

Job 23:10

You have taken account of my
wanderings;
Put my tears in Your
bottle.
Are they not in Your book?

Psalm 56:8

The Lord will accomplish
what concerns me.

Psalm 138:8

My times are in Your hand.

Psalm 31:15

AiRhead

Hope

My soul wait in silence
  for God only.
For my hope is from Him.
He only is my rock
  and my salvation,
My stronghold;
I shall not be shaken.
On God my salvation
  and my glory rest;
The rock of my strength,
  my refuge is in God.
Trust in Him at all times,
  O people
Pour out your heart before Him;
God is a refuge for us.

Psalm 62:5-8

Hope

Hearty

My flesh and my heart may fail,
But God is the strength of my heart
   and my portion forever.
                              Psalm 73:26

"I love You, O Lord, my strength."
The Lord is my rock and my fortress
   and my deliverer.
My God, my rock, in whom I take refuge.
                              Psalm 18:1-2

"The Lord is my portion,"
   says my soul,
"Therefore I have hope in Him."
                  Lamentations 3:24

Hearty

CleaveR

Cling to Him; give a squeeze!
Make it your aim
Him to please!

But you are to cling to the Lord your God.
Joshua 23:8

You shall fear the Lord your God; you
shall serve Him and cling to Him,
and you shall swear by His name
Deuteronomy 10:20

So choose life in order that
you may live, you and your
descendants, by loving the
Lord your God, by obeying
His voice, and by holding fast
to Him; for this is your life and
the length of your days.
Deuteronomy 30:19-20

My soul clings to You;
Your right hand upholds me.
Psalm 63:8

CleaveR

Consider the Lilies

Consider the lilies,
how they grow:
they neither toil nor spin;
but I tell you, not even
Solomon in all his glory
clothed himself like
one of these.
But if God so clothes the
grass in the field, which
is alive today and tomorrow
is thrown into the furnace,
how much more will He clothe
you?

Luke 12:27-28

Daisy Girl

Psalm 23

The Lord is my shepherd, I shall not want.
He makes me lie down in green pastures;
He leads me beside quiet waters.
He restores my soul;
He guides me in the paths of rightousness
for His name's sake.
Even though I walk through the valley of the
shadow of death, I fear no evil, for You are with me;
Your rod and Your staff, they comfort me.
You prepare a table before me
  in the presence of my enemies;
  You have anointed my head with oil;
  My cup overflows.
   Surely goodness and lovingkindness
    will follow me all the days of my life,
    And I will dwell in the house
     of the Lord forever.

            Psalm 23

New Sue

Kindness and Truth

Do not let kindness and truth leave you;
Bind them around your neck,
Write them on the tablet of your heart.
                                    Proverbs 3:3
You desire truth in the innermost being,
And in the hidden part You will make me
    know wisdom.   Psalm 51:6

These are the things which you should do:
    speak the truth to one another.
                                    Zechariah. 8:16

Kindness

Truth

Kind and True

Sunny

The Lord God is a sun and shield;
The Lord gives grace and glory;
No good thing does He withold
  from those who walk uprightly.
O Lord of hosts,
How blessed is the man
  who trusts in you!

Psalm 84:11-12

Sunny

Catchy Words

I fastened a tray under my chin
It was designed for my words to fall in.
The extra, the foolish, the false and unkind
At the end of the day in the tray I would find.
But before the cock crowed
The tray overflowed! *LH*

Then I said, "I am a man of
unclean lips."
Isaiah 6:5

When there are words, transgression
is unavoidable.
Proverbs 10:19

Even a fool, when he keeps silent,
is considered wise.
Proverbs 17:28

Do not be hasty in word or impulsive in
thought to bring up a matter in the
presence of God. For God is in heaven
and you are on earth; therefore let your
words be few.
Ecclesiastes 5:2

Few Words

Imaginary Muzzle

In my mind, on my mouth
I placed a muzzle.
My unseen fashion look
Taken from the Blessed Book
Intended to restrain the excess flow
Of all the countless, priceless things I know.
Rather I would listen
With open ears and heart
And love and care instead
Of showing myself smart!

I said, "I will guard my ways
That I may not sin with my tongue;
I will guard my mouth
as with a muzzle."   Psalm 39:1

Set a guard, O Lord over my mouth;
Keep watch over the door of my lips.
                                       Psalm 141:3

For the mouth speaks out of that which
which fills the heart.   Matthew 12:34

Keep your tongue from evil
and your lips from speaking deceit.
                                       Psalm 34:13
He who guards his mouth and his tongue,
Guards his soul from troubles.
                                       Proverbs 21:23

He who gives an answer before he hears,
It is folly and shame to him.
                                       Proverbs 18:13

Guarded

Soul Food

Your words were found and I ate them,
And Your words became for me a joy
   and the delight of my heart.

                       Jeremiah 15:16

How sweet are Your Words to my taste!
Yes, sweeter than honey to my mouth!
From Your precepts I get understanding.

                   Psalm 119:103

They are life to those who find them
And health to all their body.

                    Proverbs 4:22

My son, eat honey, for it is good,
Yes, the honey from the comb is
   sweet to your taste;
Know that wisdom is thus
   for your soul;
If you find it, then there
   will be a future,
And your hope will not
   be cut off.

                 Proverbs 24:13-14

Soul Food

Strength and Song

The Lord is my strength and song.

Psalm 118:14

Speak to one another in psalms and hymns and spiritual songs, singing and making melody with your heart to the Lord.

Ephesians 5:19

Be strong in the Lord and in the strength of His might.

Ephesians 6:10

Melody

Rest Easy

In peace I will both lie down and sleep,
For You alone, O Lord, make me to dwell in safety.

Psalm 4:8

I lay down and slept;
I awoke, for the Lord sustains me.

Psalm 3:5

I have set the Lord continually before me;
Because He is at my right hand, I will not be shaken.

Psalm 16:8

"He who listens to me will live securely
And will be at ease from the dread of evil."

Proverbs 1:33

Good Night

Hymns

Morning Has Broken

Morning has broken,
  like the first morning,
Blackbird has spoken,
  like the first bird.
Praise for the singing,
  praise for the morning,
Praise for them springing
  fresh from the word.

Mine is the sunlight,
  mine is the morning,
Born of the one light
  Eden saw play.
Praise with elation,
  praise every morning,
God's re-creation
  of the new day.

Eleanor Fargeon, 1931

Let the morning bring me word of
  your unfailing love, for I have put
  my trust in you.

Psalm 143:8, NIV

Happy Girl

24

Be Thou My Vision

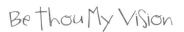

Be Thou my Vision, O Lord of my heart;
Naught be all else to me, save that Thou art.
Thou my best Thought, by day or by night,
Waking or sleeping, Thy presence my light.

Be Thou my Wisdom, and Thou my true Word;
I ever with Thee and Thou with me, Lord;
Thou my great Father, I Thy true son;
Thou in me dwelling, and I with Thee one.

Be Thou my battle Shield, Sword for the fight;
Be Thou my dignity, Thou my Delight;
Thou my soul's Shelter, Thou my high Tower:
   Raise Thou me heavenward, O Power of my power.

Riches I heed not, nor man's empty praise,
Thou mine Inheritance, now and always:
Thou and Thou only, first in my heart,
High King of Heaven, my Treasure Thou art.

High King of Heaven, my victory won,
May I reach heaven's joys, O bright Heaven's Sun!
Heart of my own heart, whatever befall,
Still be my Vision, O Ruler of all.

I pray that the eyes of your heart may be enlightened,
so that you will know what is the hope of His
calling.   Ephesians 1:18

"Regard all things in God."   Francois Fenelon, 1680

God Glasses

25

It Is Well With My Soul

When peace, like a river, attendeth my way,
When sorrows like sea billows roll;
Whatever my lot, Thou hast taught me to say,
It is well, it is well, with my soul

It is well, with my soul,
It is well, with my soul,
It is well, it is well, with my soul.

Though Satan should buffet, though trials should come,
Let this blest assurance control,
That Christ has regarded my helpless estate,
And hath shed His own
blood for my soul.

And Lord, haste the day when
my faith shall be sight,
The clouds be rolled back
as a scroll;
The trump shall resound,
and the Lord shall descend,
Even so it is well with my soul.

Horatio Spafford, 1873

Return to your rest, O my soul.
Psalm 116:7

Bella

26

Praise to the Lord the Almighty

Praise to the Lord, the Almighty, the King of creation!
O my soul, praise Him, for He is thy health and salvation!
All ye who hear now to His temple draw near;
Praise Him in glad adoration.

Praise to the Lord, Who over all things so wonderously reigneth,
Shelters thee under His wings, yea, so gently sustaineth!
Hast thou not seen how thy desires ever have been
Granted in what He ordaineth?

Praise to the Lord, O let
    all that is in me adore him!
All that hath life and breath,
    come now with praises
    before Him.
Let the Amen sound
    from His people again,
    Gladly for aye we
    adore Him.

Joachim Neander, 1680

I will sing praise to the Lord
as long as I live.
                    Psalm 104:33

Rhapsody

27

What a Friend We Have in Jesus

What a friend we have in Jesus,
All our sins and griefs to bear!
What a privilege to carry
Everything to God in prayer!
O what peace we often forfeit,
O what needless pain we bear,
All because we do not carry
Everything to God in prayer!

Have we trials and temptations?
Is there trouble anywhere?
We should never be discouraged;
Take it to the Lord in prayer.
Can we find a friend so faithful
Who will all our sorrows share?
Jesus knows our every weakness;
Take it to the Lord in prayer.

Are we weak and heavy laden,
Cumbered with a load of care?
Precious Saviour, still our refuge
Take it to the Lord in prayer.
Do your friends despise, forsake you?
Take it to the Lord in prayer!
In His arms He'll take and shield you,
You will find a solace there.

Joseph M. Scriven, 1855

But I have called you friends.
John 15:15

Count Your Blessings

When upon life's billows you are tempest tossed,
When you are discouraged, thinking all is lost,
Count your many blessings, name them one by one,
And it will surprise you what the Lord hath done.

Count your blessings, name them one by one,
Count your blessings, see what God hath done!
Count your blessings, name them one by one,
Count your many blessings, see what God hath done.

Are you ever burdened with a load of care?
Does the cross seem heavy you are called to bear?
Count your many blessings, every doubt will fly,
And you will be singing as the days go by.

So, amid the conflict whether great or small,
Do not be discouraged, God is over all;
Count your many blessings,
    angels will attend,
Help and comfort give you
    to your journey's end.

Johnson Oatman, 1856

Every good thing given and
every perfect gift is from above.

James 1:17

29

All Creatures of Our God and King

All creatures of our God and King
Lift up your voice and with us sing,
Alleluia! Alleluia!
Thou burning sun with golden beam,
Thou silver moon with softer gleam!
O praise Him! O praise Him!
Alleluia! Alleluia! Alleluia!

Thou rushing wind that art so strong
Ye clouds that sail in Heaven along,
Oh praise Him! Alleluia!
Thou rising morn, in praise rejoice,
Ye lights of evening, find a voice
O praise Him! O praise Him!
Alleluia! Alleluia! Alleluia!

And all ye men of tender heart,
Forgiving others, take your part,
O sing ye! Alleluia!
Ye who long pain and sorrow bear,
Praise God and on Him cast your care!
O praise Him! O praise Him!
Alleluia! Alleluia!.Alleluia!

Let all things their Creator bless,
And worship Him in humbleness,
O praise Him! Alleluia!
Praise, praise the Father, praise the Son,
And praise the Spirit, Three in One
O praise Him! O praise Him!
Allelulia! Allelulia! Alleluia!

St Francis of Assisi, 1225

All Creatures of Our God and King
Praise Medley

All plants and flowers lively say,
Dressed every day in His array
O praise Him! O praise Him!
Burning tomorrow in the flame,
Beauty today we praise His name!
Alleluia! Alleluia! Alleluia!

Ye birds on wing joyfully sing;
Sing praises to our God and King
O praise Him! O praise Him!
Thou mighty rivers, sea rejoice,
Thy rushing waters be His voice
O praise Him! O praise Him! Alleluia!

These hands with artful work be filled
Today to do His way, His will!
O praise Him! O praise Him!
Let everything that hath breath praise,
Sing alleluia all our days!
O praise Him! O praise Him! Alleluia!

My need for refuge, peace I bring;
I will dwell safely 'neath His wing.
How I praise Him! How I praise Him!
Alleluia! Alleluia!

In sunshine on the flowery vale,
In thunderstorm and fearsome gale
I will praise Him! I will praise Him!
Lord all my trouble, fears I bring,
As a waistband Lord I cling.
Alleluia! Jeremiah 13:11

Lord in Your kindness do forgive,
Lord by Your Spirit in me live.
Alleluia! Romans 8:11
On my way to heaven!
On my way to heaven!

Morning, noon and evening I will pray;
Cry aloud unto Him every day.
And He will hear my voice,
He will hear my voice.
Alleluia! Psalm 55:17

All men on bended knee shall bring
Praise, honor glory to the King!
Alleluia! Alleluia!
First, Last, Beginning and the End;
Alpha and Omega is our friend.
Alleluia! Alleluia!
Praise Jehovah! Praise Jehovah!

©Loralie Harris, 2018

Praise Him, sun and moon;
Praise Him all stars of light!
Psalm 148:3
Let everything that has breath praise the Lord.
Praise the Lord!   Psalm 150:6

Evening and morning and at noon, I will complain and murmur,
And He will hear my voice.   Psalm 55:17

31

Guide Me, O Thou Great Jehovah

Guide me, O Thou great Jehovah,
Pilgrim through this barren land.
I am weak, but Thou art mighty;
Hold me with Thy powerful hand.
Bread of Heaven, Bread of Heaven,
Feed me till I want no more;
Feed me till I want no more.

Open now the crystal fountain,
Whence the healing stream doth flow;
Let the fire and cloudy pillar
Lead me all my journey through.
Strong Deliverer, strong Deliverer,
Be Thou still my Strength and Shield;
Be Thou still my Strength and Shield.

William Williams, 1745

Blessed are those whose strength
is in You, whose hearts are set
on pilgrimage.

Psalm 84:5, NIV

Pilgrimette

Great Is Thy Faithfulness

Great is Thy faithfulness, O God my Father,
There is no shadow of turning with Thee;
Thou changest not, Thy compassions, they fail not;
As Thou hast been, Thou forever will be.

Summer and winter, and springtime and harvest,
Sun, moon, and stars in their courses above,
Join with all nature in manifold witness
To Thy great faithfulness, mercy and love.

Pardon for Sin and a peace
   that endureth,
Thine own dear presence
   to cheer and to guide,
Strength for today
   and bright hope for tomorrow
Blessings all mine,
   with ten thousand beside!

Great is Thy faithfulness!
Great is Thy faithfulness!
Morning by morning new mercies I see;
All I have needed Thy hand hath provided;
Great is Thy faithfulness, Lord unto me!

Thomas Chisholm, 1923

The Lord's lovingkindnesses indeed never cease,
for His compassions never fail. They are new
every morning; great is Your faithfulness.

Lamentations 3:22-23

Sing

Blessed Assurance

Blessed assurance, Jesus is mine!
O what a foretaste of glory divine!
Heir of salvation, purchase of God,
Born of His Spirit, washed in His blood.

This is my story, this is my song,
Praising my Savior all the day long;
This is my story, this is my song,
Praising my Savior all the day long.

Perfect submission, all is at rest;
I in my Savior am happy and blest.
Watching and waiting, looking above,
Filled with His goodness, lost in His love.

This is my story, this is my song,
Praising my Savior all the day long;
This is my story, this is my song,
Praising my Savior all the day long.

Fanny Crosby, 1873

God is our refuge and strength,
A very present help in trouble.   Psalm 46:1

To PondeR

tHe Voice of CReation

On the point of the picket the little bird perched
Basking in the morning sun.
His feathers and his feet, his beak and his song
All to the Master belong.
The flower below spreads wide its petals
Thrusting a thousand stamens to the sky,
In honor of the Master on high.
The carpet of grass, every sprig, every blade
Sings, "By the Master I was made!"
And the willow tree bows in humble adoration
Giving praise to the Lord of Creation.

Listen, and you will hear, the cottage garden speak out loud;
Conversing with the sun and the cloud.
Asking, "Where is the man, the crown of creation;
Why does he not join us in this conversation?"
Then the cloud said to the sun, "What we are, we will be,
But God, for His purpose, made the man free;
Free to walk with Him, free to walk away.
Since creation, that's how it's been until this day."

Then the willow began to weep, and the grass could hardly keep
From crying, "What shall we dew?"
Then the sun said, "I will shine!" And the bird said, "I will sing!"
And the flower said, "All my beauty I will bring!
Together today, we will call to the man
To bring him to the King, to the Master, if we can!"

The heavens declare the glory of God;
the skies proclaim the work of his hands.

Psalm 19:1, NIV

For since the creation of the world His invisible attributes, His
eternal power and divine nature, have been clearly seen, being
understood through what has been made.

Romans 1:20

BiRd WatcheR

Storms of Life

The clouds are blowing over;
The sunshine is returning.
The air is calm again
After turbulance and churning.
Like the storm that's passing,
The winds of life harassing,
Lord haste the day,
Eternal light
When all things
You will put right.

"He will wipe away every tear from their eyes;
and there will no longer be any death; there will no
longer be any mourning, or crying, or pain; the first
things have passed away."

                                    Revelation 21:4

FeatheRed FRiends

Birds of a feather, that's how we roll,
Though life's kicks and punches take their toll;
Through all kinds of weather, whatever it be,
We'll stick together you and me.

When the storms roll in, through thick and thin,
When joys elate and life's a grin;
No matter how long, how far we're apart,
You'll always be there, alive in my heart.

Yes, birds of a feather, and so we agree
As we walk this sod,
I to you, you to me;
Precious, sweet gift from God.

Behold, how good and how pleasant it is
For brothers to dwell together in unity!

Psalm 133:1

To Ruthie

I wish you would have told me
Before that fateful day;
What was on your heart and mind,
The things you had to say.

Instead, out of the blue it came-
Stored up anger, hurt, blame.

Have I reached the limit
Of your love for me?
Have I stretched your heart
To it's capacity?
I know I'm not behaving
The way you think I should.
I pray you will forgive today;
I am but made of clay.

Therefore, laying aside falsehood, speak truth each
one of you with his neighbor, for we are members of
one another. Be angry, and yet do not sin; do not
let the sun go down on your anger, and do not give
the devil an opportunity.

Ephesians 4:25-27

For we all stumble in many ways.　　James 3:2

Bearing with one another, and forgiving
each other, whoever has a complaint
against anyone; just as the Lord
forgave you, so also should you.

Colossians 3:13

The Bright Side of Blue

Seems blue to me
So many things I see;
Sorrow, loss and pain;
Instead of sunshine, rain.
But blue's not so bad;
Consider just a tad;
All the lovely things of blue
God made for me and you.

Bachelor Buttons bob and bounce;
Blue and black, brightly announce
The month of May, hear them say,
"We hope you have a lovely day!"
Popcorn clouds passing by
Way up high the open sky,
Where I will fly by and by.
Shimmering lake where I take
A restful recreation break,
Sapphire bright beams of light,
Sweet blue birds in flight.

Yes, many lovely things of blue
Waiting there for me and you.
When we're sad, it's not as bad
If we consider just a tad,
All the lovely things of blue
God made for me and you.

Betty Blue

41

Comeback!

Hats off to you!
After all you've been through,
Now may all of your dreams come true!
May your strength be more
Than it was before,
And may God's good blessing
Visit your door.
May He give you direction,
His perfect selection
Of good things to do
With your life, all the rest.
Days foul or fair, many or few,
May others by you be blessed.
May you emerge a new "you" less fettered
By the pain and the trouble made better.

Blessed is the man who perseveres
under trial; for once he has been
approved, he will receive the crown
of life which the Lord has promised
to those who love Him.
James 1:12

Consider it all joy, my brethren,
when you encounter various trials,
knowing that the testing of your
faith produces endurance.
James 1:2

Comeback!

Hollyhocks

I love to think of hollyhocks
Of fluffy blooms on hardy stalks.
Piercing through the summer blue,
Lettuce leaves and charming hue;
Peeking o'er the picket point
Passers by to anoint.
With color, beauty for the day
Send them lifted on their way!

Then they fade and die away,
But they'll be back another day;
Plump seed pods guarantee,
"You've not seen the last of me!
Lord willing, I'll be back next year
To lift your heart and bring you cheer!"

Sleeping Beauty

They slumber now but soon will wake,
Their first breath of season take.
Shower, sun will call them forth;
To grace the alleyway and porch.
Lovely leaves and petals call,
"Look at me! One and all!"
Gift of beauty, gift from God
Sleeping now beneath the sod.

As for man, his days are like grass; As a flower of the
field, so he flourishes. When the wind has passed over
it, it is no more, And its place acknowledges it no longer.
But the lovingkindness of the Lord is from everlasting
to everlasting on those who fear Him.

Psalm 103:15-17

Holy Mallow (sweet gift from God)

Not to Worry

From Psalm 37 a list for you
Instead of fretting so much, we can do:
Trust God, do good,
Act like we should,
Delight in Him day and night, and do right;
Commit your way to Him every day.
Be patient, calm down
When you look all around.
Don't be mad, but be glad;
God's in control,
And with life's punches roll.

Then in the end the bad guys won't be there,
Their memory, not even a trace
Yes, in the end, only God's friends,
And all pain and injustice He will erase.

T R W C D D D F F F F

Trust	Dwell
Rest	Do Good
Wait	Delight in the Lord
Commit	Forsake wrath
	Fret not
	Feed on His Faithfulness

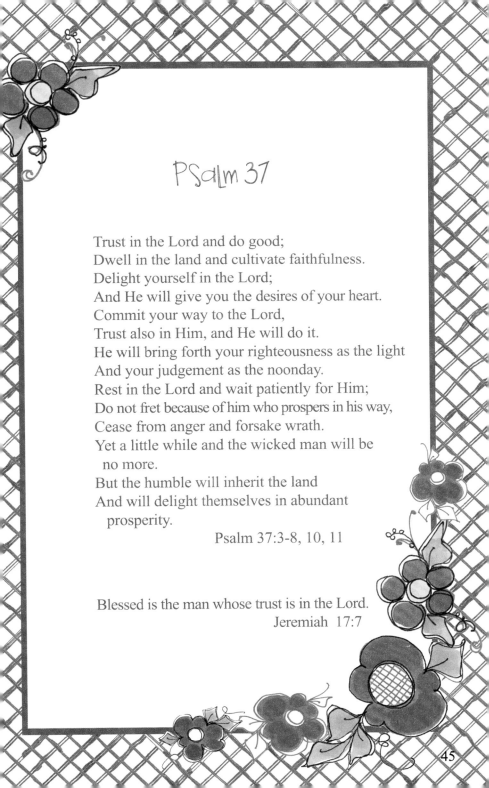

PSalm 37

Trust in the Lord and do good;
Dwell in the land and cultivate faithfulness.
Delight yourself in the Lord;
And He will give you the desires of your heart.
Commit your way to the Lord,
Trust also in Him, and He will do it.
He will bring forth your righteousness as the light
And your judgement as the noonday.
Rest in the Lord and wait patiently for Him;
Do not fret because of him who prospers in his way,
Cease from anger and forsake wrath.
Yet a little while and the wicked man will be
  no more.
But the humble will inherit the land
And will delight themselves in abundant
  prosperity.

Psalm 37:3-8, 10, 11

Blessed is the man whose trust is in the Lord.

Jeremiah 17:7

BLOSSOM

In her straw bonnet
With bright posies on it
She makes her way
To her garden each day.
She waters and weeds,
Tends to their needs;
With her sweet flowers,
She can spend hours!
Then when she leaves
Some sweet garden cleaves
To her mind and her heart,
To the day such a start!

And the longer she stays
The more she will praise
The Maker of flowers,
The Ancient of Days.

And the Lord God took
the man and put him into
the garden of Eden to
cultivate it and keep it.
Genesis 2:15

BLOSSOM

46

The Promise

Am I safe to love you? Will you always stay?
In the end, be the friend, you are to me today?
Can I trust you through the years
With my joys, my tears and fears?
Can I with you always be true?
Always be always me?

Will you forgive me when I fail?
Stay with me in calm and gale?
Will you keep me when I'm down?
Share with me when good comes 'round?

My heart's desire, and so I pray
You'll stay the friend you are to me today.

You are safe to love me, I will always stay.
In the end, I'll be the friend I am to you today.
You can trust me through the years
With your joys, your tears and fears.
You can with me always be, always true, always you.

I will forgive you when you fail.
I'll stay with you in calm and gale.
I will keep you when you're down;
I'll share with you when good comes round.
My desire, and so I pray
By God's grace your friend I'll stay.

Am I safe to love you? Will you always stay?
In the end, be the friend, you are to me today?
In days ahead when times get tough,
Real life sets in with serious stuff,
Remind me of this day of love
When I promised to the end, I would be your best friend.

Though the winds of change may blow;
The way ahead we do not know.
Will you say to me today,
I'll go with you all the way?

And when our little boat is rocked
By life's storms is turned and tossed,
Together we will stay the course
In the gale against the force
Of life troubles, ups-and-downs,
Then celebrate when good comes round.

Yes, I will say to you today, by God's grace, your friend I'll stay.

Floral Affection

Pretty Stormy

47

Phantom Phobia

I had a phantom phobia
Come visit me today.
It knocked me down
And rolled me round;
It took my joy away.
In the midst of my days doing,
On my heart and mind 'a chewing;
The nerve it had, my peace stealing;
With fear and trembling I went reeling;
With all I had to my faith clinging!

Then I heard a still small voice
Speak to me, "Make this choice,
Underneath My wing be clinging
In your heart, to Me be singing
All your cares, to Me be bringing.
Delight yourself in Me, you'll see
From the phantom you'll be free."

I sought the Lord, and He answered me,
And delivered me from all my fears.   Psalm 34:4

Be gracious to me, O God, be gracious to me,
For my soul takes refuge in You;
And in the shadow of Your wings I will take refuge
Until destruction passes by.   Psalm 57:1-2

Out of the depths I have cried to You, O Lord.
Lord, hear my voice!   Psalm 130:1

Hear my prayer, O Lord, and give ear to my cry.
                                 Psalm 39:12

When my anxious thoughts multiply within me,
Your consolations delight my soul.   Psalm 94:19

FeaRLeSS

48

Heap o' Notions

In her head, a heap o'notions,
A frenzied, chaotic emotion commotion.
Through the years she collected
In her psyche hid, protected
Events, comments, perhaps well meant,
Through the years her self had bent.
Her private intake, gone unchecked
Became habit and reflex.
Unbeknownst to her
This cache became her purr.

And every day this collection,
Glory be! Resurrection!
Up to meet each new event,
Experience, off-hand comment
Mixed together, a powerful brew
Over which to chew and stew.

Colored, shaped and formed today
By long ago and far away.

Lord, give me eyes to see;
By Your Spirit, extricate me
Wretched man that I am
Help me Lord! I know You can!
Kindly grant me grace today
To bend, incline my heart Your way.

Heap o'Notions

Be transformed by the renewing of your mind.
Romans 12:2

Incline my heart to your testimonies.
Psalm 119:2

Wretched man that I am! Who will set me free
from the body of this death?
Romans 7:24

49

Love is...

Patient

Kind

Not jealous

Does not brag

Is not arrogant

Does not act unbecomingly

Does not seek it's own

Is not provoked

Does not take into account a wrong suffered

Does not rejoice in unrighteousness

Rejoices in the truth

Bears all things

Believes all things

Hopes all things

Endures all things

Love never fails

Love is patient, love is kind and is not jealous; love does not brag and is not arrogant, does not act unbecomingly; it does not seek its own, is not provoked, does not take into account a wrong suffered, does not rejoice in unrighteousness, but rejoices in the truth; bears all things, believes all things, hopes all things, endures all things. Love never fails . . .

1 Corinthians 13: 4-8

In the Morning

Heavenly Father, I cry out!
I cannot live without
Your precious presence
Every minute.
This day kindly,
Lord be in it.
Morning, noon and night
Be my hearing, thought and sight;
And late tonight
When weary I
On my pillow lie,
Thoughts of You
Will bring me through
To meet tomorrow
Fresh and new.

Let the morning bring me word of Your
unfailing love, for I have put my trust in you.
                                    Psalm 143:8, NIV

In the morning I will order my prayer to You
    and eagerly watch.
                                    Psalm 5:3

He gives to His beloved even in his sleep.
                                    Psalm 127:2

Stepping Stones

Across the stream of life I go
On stepping stones beneath the flow;
From one to the next,
The way I do not know.
As the end of each comes into view,
Lord for the next I look to You.
For my life's journey out ahead,
Lord I look to You instead
Of fretting, sweating, letting
Fear grip my heart and mind;
Instead I know across this flow,
In You my way I'll find
Beneath my feet as I walk
Faithful, loving, eternal Rock!

The mind of man plans his
way, But the Lord directs
his steps.

Proverbs 16:9

"The Rock! His work is perfect,
 For all His ways are just;
A God of faithfulness and without injustice,
Righteous and upright is He."

Deuteronomy 32:4

Steppin' Out

Home up Yonder

Change of Address

When I get up yonder
At last I will be home.
Finally! Enough for me,
The universe to roam!

Lord, thank You for this hope.
'Til then my heart will be
Striving, struggling every day
To find my rest in Thee.

"Cease striving and know that I am God."   Psalm 46:10

But according to His promise we are looking for new
heavens and a new earth, in which righteousness dwells.
                                                        2 Peter 3:13

This hope we have as an anchor of the soul.   Hebrews 6:19

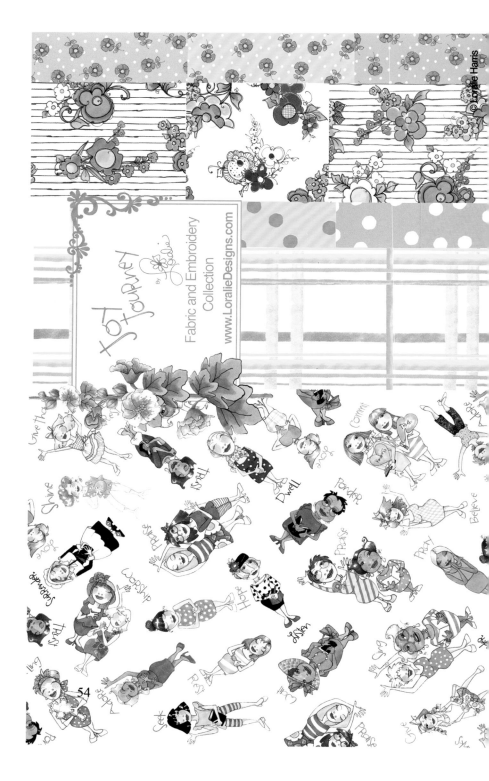